Christmas

COLLECTION

18 festive pieces for Manuals

Kevin Mayhew

We hope you enjoy the music in *Christmas Collection for Manuals*.
Further copies of this and our many other books are available
from your local music shop or Christian bookshop.

In case of difficulty, please contact the publisher direct by writing to:

The Sales Department
KEVIN MAYHEW LTD
Rattlesden
Bury St Edmunds
Suffolk IP30 0SZ

Phone 01449 737978
Fax 01449 737834
E-mail info@kevinmayhewltd.com

Please ask for our complete catalogue of outstanding Church Music.

Front Cover: *The Nativity* (detail) by Giotto Di Bondone (*c.* 1266-1337).
Courtesy of Arena Chapel, Cappella Degli Scrovegni,
Padua, Italy/SuperStock Ltd, London.
Reproduced by kind permission.

Cover designed by Angela Staley.

First published in Great Britain in 1998 by Kevin Mayhew Ltd.

ISBN 1 84003 246 4
ISMN M 57004 436 8
Catalogue No: 1400183

0 1 2 3 4 5 6 7 8 9

Music Editor: Donald Thomson
Music setting by Vernon Turner

Printed and bound in Great Britain

Contents

About the Composers

Malcolm Archer (*b*.1952) is Organist and Master of the Choristers at Wells Cathedral. He is conductor of the Wells Oratorio Society and the City of Bristol Choir. In addition to his work as a composer and conductor, he leads a busy life as an organ recitalist.

Rosalie Bonighton (*b*.1946) is a recitalist, teacher and composer with a special interest in writing music for new liturgical needs.

Simon Clark (*b*.1975) has studied composition with many prominent English composers, including Howard Blake and Michael Finnissy. He is active in Sussex musical circles and takes a keen interest in the musical life of St Mary the Virgin Church, Hartfield.

Adrian Vernon Fish (*b*.1956) studied composition with Alan Ridout and Herbert Howells. His output is considerable, ranging from symphonies and organ music to cantatas and cabaret songs.

Andrew Fletcher (*b*.1950) is a teacher, composer, accompanist and recitalist, performing regularly all over the world.

Andrew Gant (*b*.1963) studied at St John's College, Cambridge, where he was a choral scholar, and the Royal Academy of Music in London. He is Director of Music in Chapel at Selwyn College, Cambridge, and regularly tours with the choir, recently visiting Sweden, the USA and Italy. He is Organist and Master of the Choir at the Royal Military Chapel (the Guards' Chapel), Wellington Barracks, London, and teaches composition, harmony and counterpoint at the University of Cambridge.

Richard Lloyd (*b*.1933) was Assistant Organist of Salisbury Cathedral and successively Organist of Hereford and Durham Cathedrals. He now divides his time between examining and composing.

John Marsh (*b*.1939), formerly Organist and Director of Music at St Mary Redcliffe Church, Bristol, is now a member of the music staff at Clifton College, Bristol.

Colin Mawby (*b*.1936) composes in many forms. He was previously Choral Director at Radio Telefís Éireann, the national broadcasting authority in the Republic of Ireland, and Master of the Music at Westminster Cathedral. He was recently appointed Conductor of the National Chamber Choir of Ireland, which is Ireland's only full-time, professional choir.

Andrew Moore (*b*.1954) is parish priest of Lambourn and Hungerford.

June Nixon is Organist and Director of the Choir at St Paul's Cathedral, Melbourne, Australia. She also teaches at the Melbourne University School of Music.

Richard Pantcheff (*b*.1959) is an organist and composer currently working in Oxford. Many of his works are written for the Episcopal Church of Christ the King, Frankfurt, Germany, as Composer in Association.

James Patten (*b*.1936) is a composer and conductor who has held a variety of lecturing posts at Universities and Colleges, including Professor of Composition at Trinity College of Music.

Richard Proulx (*b*.1937) is a composer, conductor and organist. He was Music Director at the Cathedral of the Holy Name in Chicago for fourteen years. His ensemble, The Cathedral Singers, is well known for its series of recordings of both early music and original works.

Betty Roe (*b*.1930) studied at the Royal Academy of Music and later with Lennox Berkeley. She composes in many forms from solo songs to operas.

Martin Setchell (*b*.1949) is an English-born and trained musician, choral conductor and organ recitalist now working in New Zealand, where he is Senior Lecturer in Music at the University of Christchurch and Organist at the Christchurch Town Hall.

Quentin Thomas (*b*.1972) was formerly Head Chorister of Westminster Abbey, music scholar at King's School, Canterbury, organ scholar at Hertford College, Oxford, and Deputy Director of Music at the Oratory School, near Reading. He is currently studying for a Master's degree in composition at the Guildhall School of Music and Drama, London, and is also active as a conductor and performer.

Stanley Vann (*b*.1910) was successively Organist at Chelmsford and Peterborough Cathedrals.

HODIE CHRISTUS NATUS EST

Colin Mawby

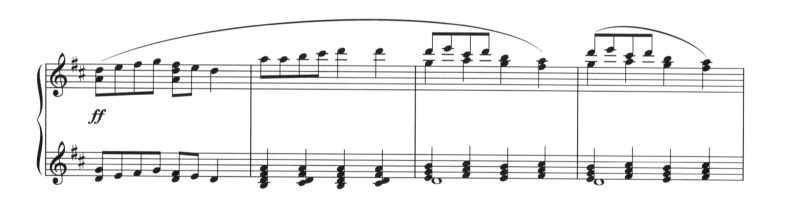

THE SHEPHERDS' LULLABY

Andrew Moore

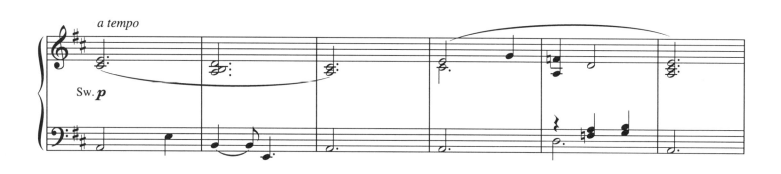

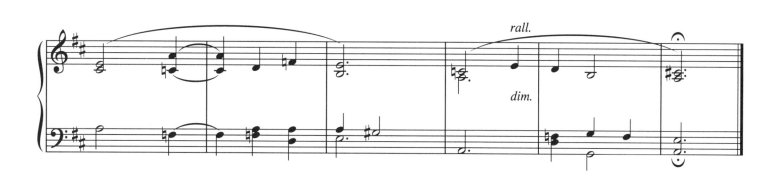

NOWELL! NOWELL! CHRISTUS NATUS EST!

Andrew Fletcher

For Nathaniel

BETHLEHEM LULLABY

Malcolm Archer

A CHRISTMAS FUGUE

Richard Pantcheff

These quavers may be sustained slightly, to create a form of echo effect

TO BETHLEHEM

James Patten

DANCING DAY

Rosalie Bonighton

2nd time to Coda

poco meno mosso   a tempo

Sw.   Gt.   Sw.   Gt. *mf*

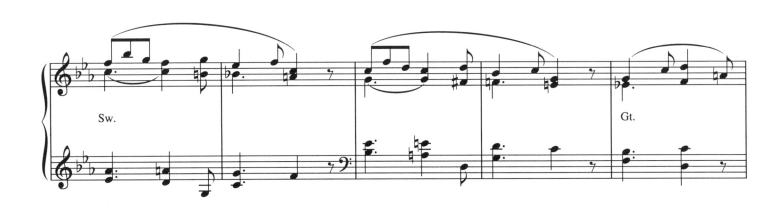

Sw.   Gt.

D.C. al Coda

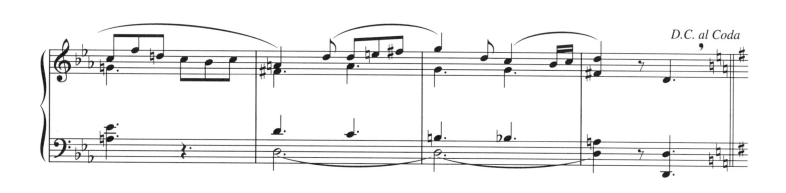

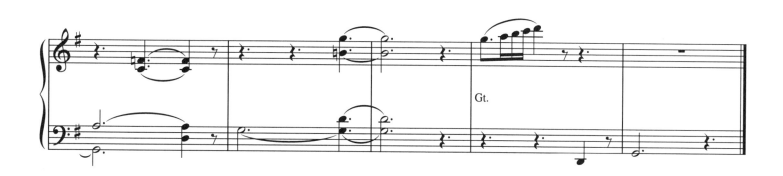

23

To William Chouinard, in admiration

VARIANTS ON 'JOYS SEVEN'

Richard Proulx

VARIATION 1

VARIATION 2

(♩ = c.104)

Flutes 8', 2'

* *Fix with a keyweight or pencil*

(Unfix)

VARIATION 3

VARIATION 4

Flutes 8', 4' **mp**
Viole 8'

VARIATION 5

($\quad$ = c.72)

Cornet 8', 4',   2⅔' 1⅗'

28

THE ANGELS' LULLABY

Andrew Gant

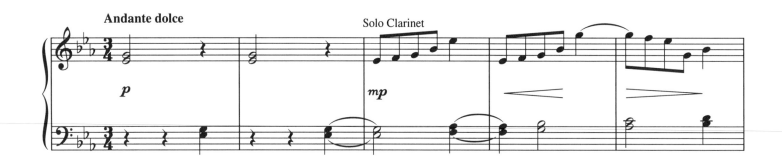

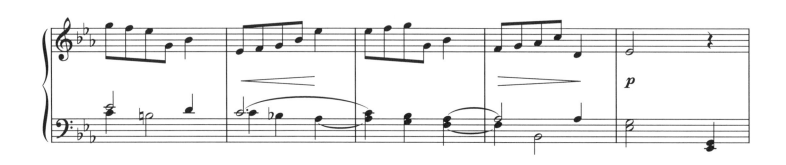

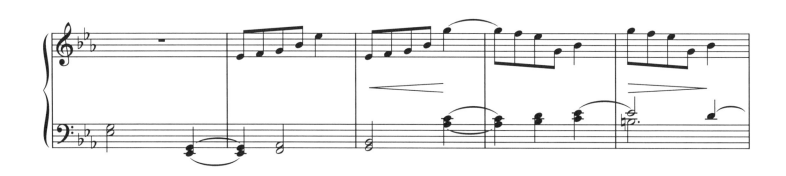

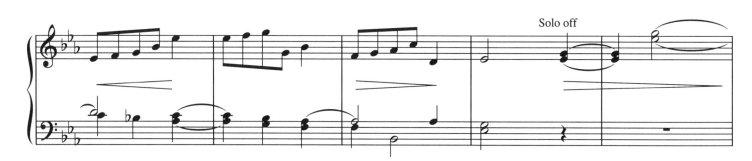

Solo
Bassoon ***mp***

p

Gt.

Solo off ***mp***

p

dim.

rit.

p

IMPROVISATION ON
'CHRISTE, REDEMPTOR OMNIUM'

Adrian Vernon Fish

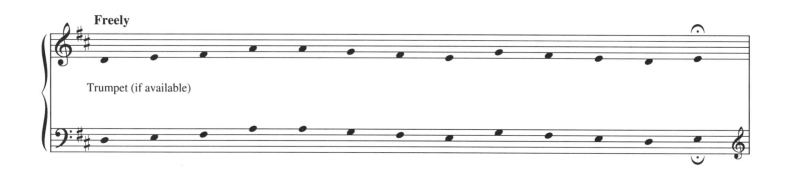

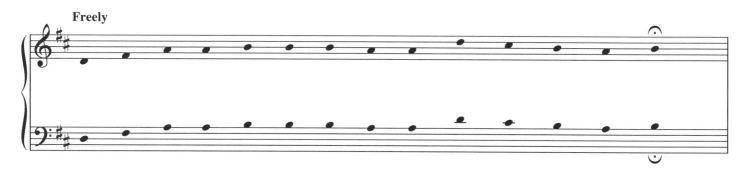

Tempo I

Freely

Tempo I

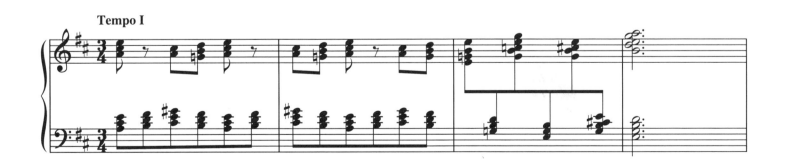

For Peter Kerr

PRELUDE FOR CHRISTMAS EVE IN TANEY

Betty Roe

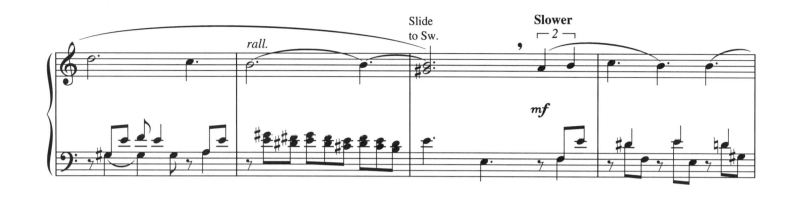

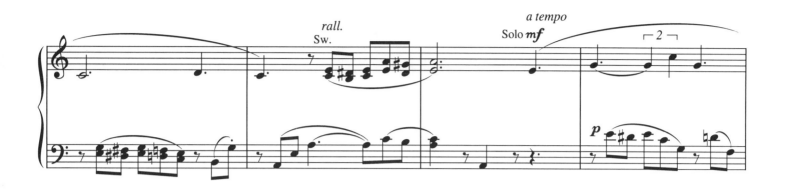

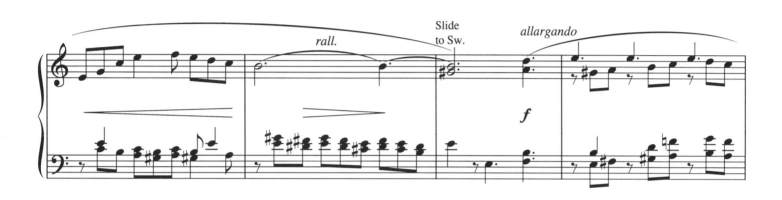

LULLABY

Richard Lloyd

IMPROVISATION ON
'ANGELS WE HAVE HEARD ON HIGH'

Simon Clark

HASTEN TO BETHLEHEM

John Marsh

rall.   *a tempo*

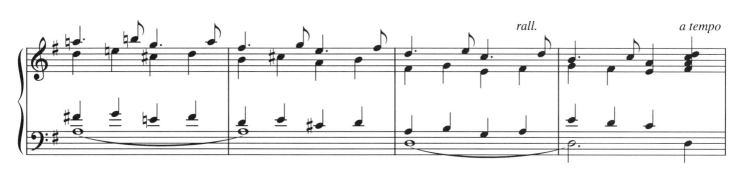

A ROUNDELAY FOR CHRISTMAS DAY

Stanley Vann

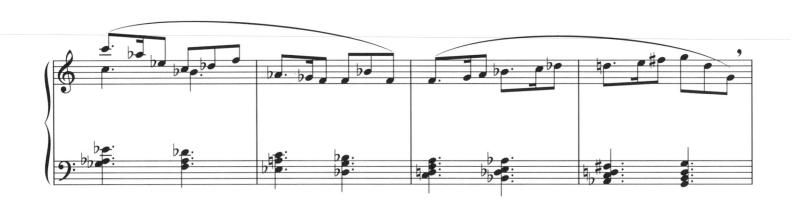

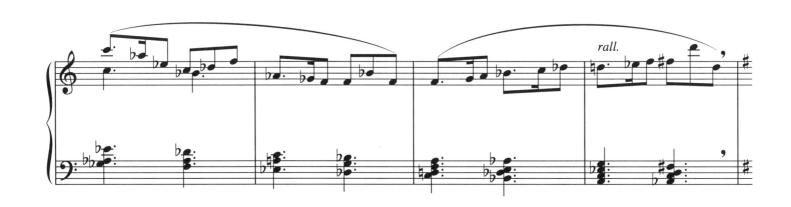

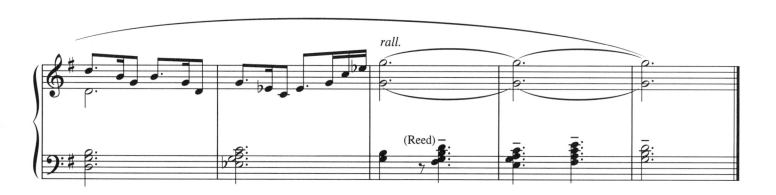

SONG OF CRADLE LOVE

Quentin Thomas

VARIATIONS ON 'HUMILITY'

June Nixon

VARIATION 1
L'istesso tempo (♩. = 92)

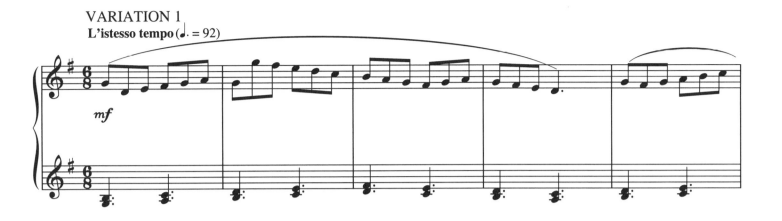

pochiss. rit.   *a tempo*

rit.

VARIATION 2
Grazioso (♩ = 84)

VARIATION 3
Agitato (♩ = 76)

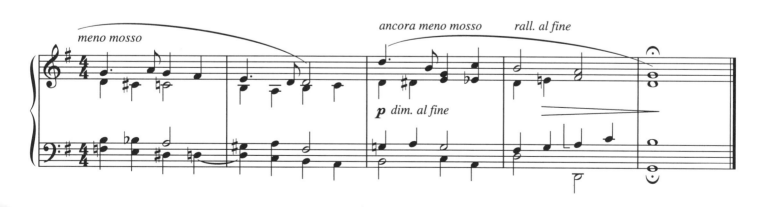

TOCCATA ON 'I SAW THREE SHIPS'

Martin Setchell